ANDREW LLOYD WEBBER'S™

T0059000

The PHANTOM of the OPERA

Music by ANDREW LLOYD WEBBER
Lyrics by CHARLES HART
Additional Lyrics by RICHARD STILGOE
Title Song: Lyrics by CHARLES HART
Additional Lyrics by RICHARD STILGOE & MIKE BATT
Book by RICHARD STILGOE & ANDREW LLOYD WEBBER

The Phantom played by MICHAEL CRAWFORD
Christine played by SARAH BRIGHTMAN   Raoul played by STEVE BARTON

Andrew Lloyd Webber™ is a trademark owned by Andrew Lloyd Webber

ISBN 978-0-7935-0374-2

7777 W. BLUEMOUND RD. P.O. BOX 13819 MILWAUKEE, WI 53213

For all works contained herein:
Unauthorized copying, arranging, adapting, recording, Internet posting, public performance,
or other distribution of the printed music in this publication is an infringement of copyright.
Infringers are liable under the law.

Cover artwork by Dewynters Limited, London

World Premiere at Her Majesty's Theatre
Thursday, October 9th, 1986

The Musical works contained in this edition may not be publicly performed in a dramatic form or
context except under license from The Really Useful Group Limited, 22 Tower street, London WC2H 9NS

Visit Hal Leonard Online at
www.halleonard.com

CONTENTS

Think Of Me

Electronic Organs
Upper: Flutes (or Tibias) 16', 4'
Lower: String 8', Reed 4'
Pedal: 16', 8'
Vib./Trem.: On, Fast

Drawbar Organs
Upper: 80 0800 000
Lower: (00) 4004 010
Pedal: 24
Vib./Trem.: On, Fast

Music by Andrew Lloyd Webber
Lyrics by Charles Hart
Additional Lyrics by Richard Stilgoe

Allegretto

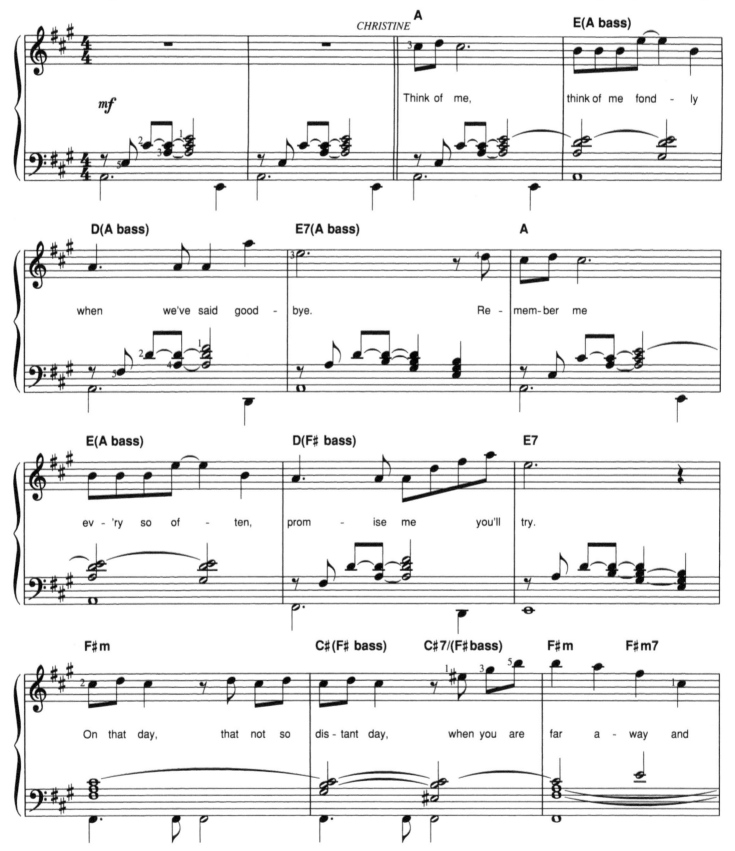

© Copyright 1986 Andrew Lloyd Webber licensed to The Really Useful Group Ltd.
International Copyright Secured   All Rights Reserved

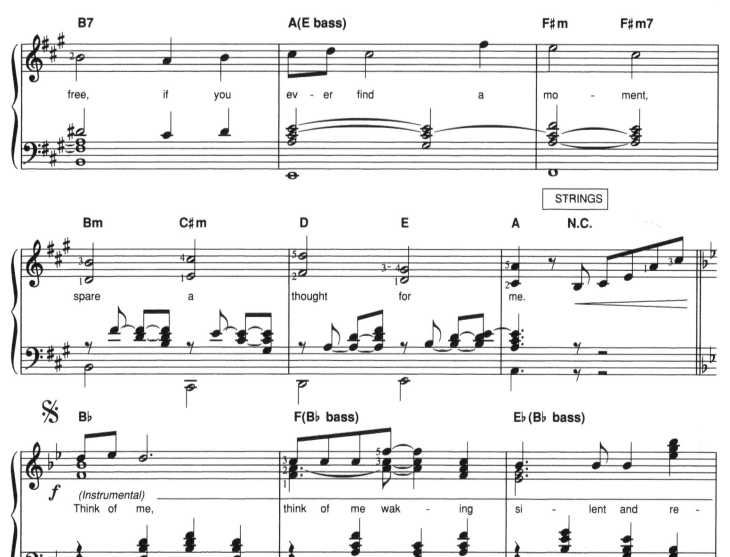

STRINGS

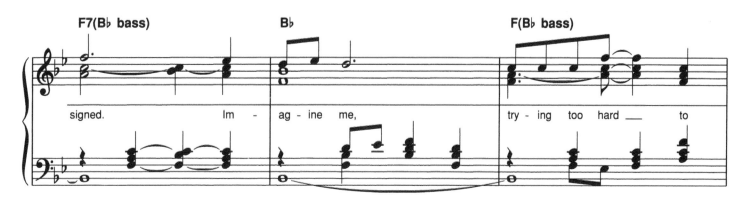

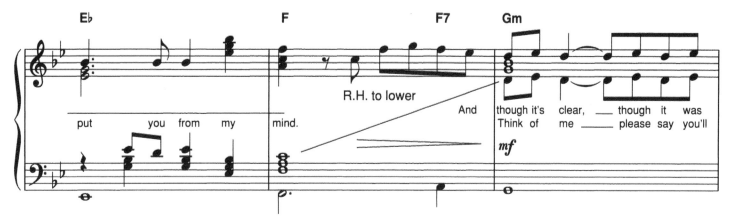

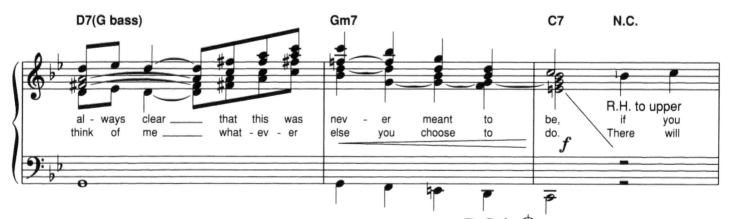

al - ways clear ____ that this was nev - er meant to be, if you
think of me ____ what - ev - er else you choose to do. There will

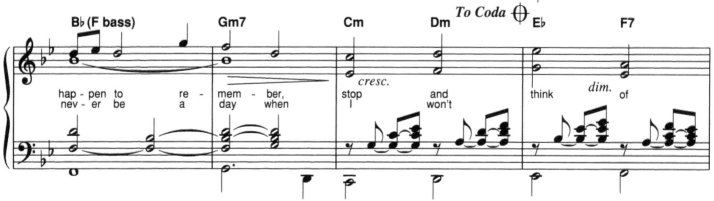

hap - pen to re - mem - ber, stop and won't think of
nev - er be a day when

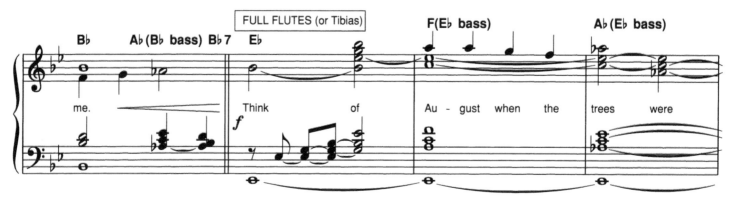

FULL FLUTES (or Tibias)

me. Think of Au - gust when the trees were

D.S. al Coda

green; don't think a - bout the way things might have been.

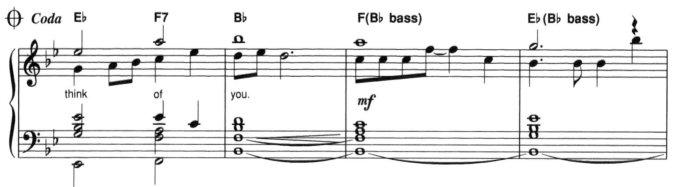

think of you.

STRINGS

RAOUL

F(B♭ bass)   B♭   F(B♭ bass)

L.H. to upper

Can it be, can it be Christ - ine?

mp

E♭   F7   Gm

Long a - go, _____ it seems so

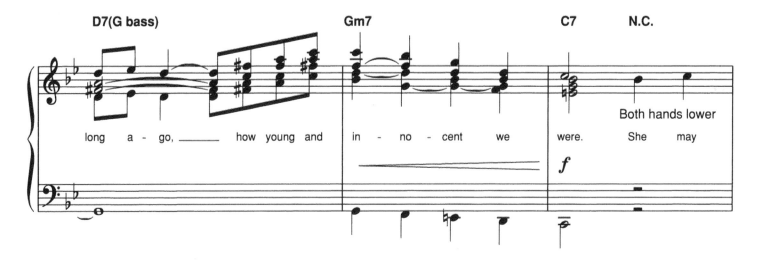

D7(G bass)   Gm7   C7   N.C.

Both hands lower

long a - go, _____ how young and in - no - cent we were. She may

f

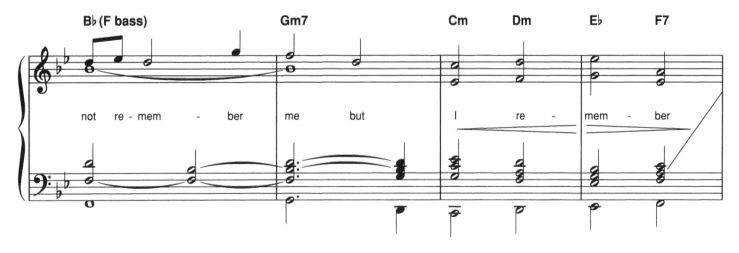

B♭ (F bass)   Gm7   Cm   Dm   E♭   F7

not re - mem - ber me but I re - mem - ber

FULL ORGAN

CHRISTINE

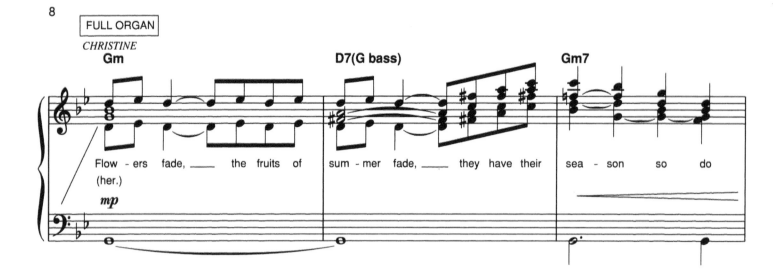

Flow - ers fade, ____ the fruits of sum - mer fade, ____ they have their sea - son so do
(her.)

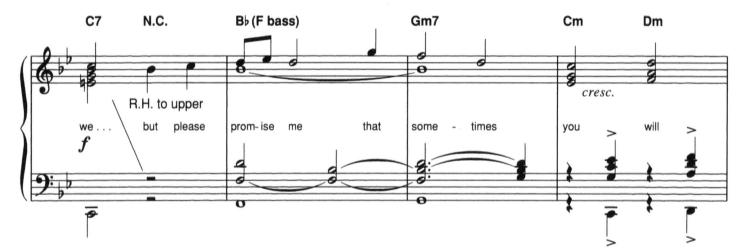

we . . . but please prom - ise me that some - times you will

Cadenza (ad lib)

think ah ____

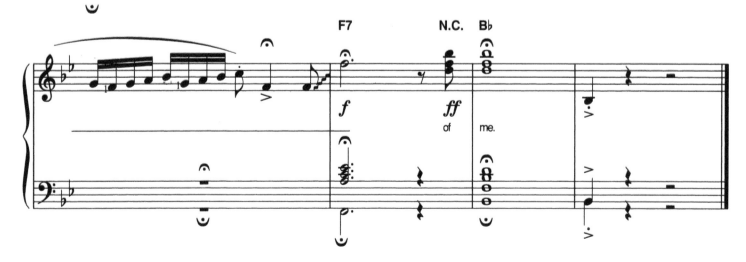

of me.

Angel Of Music

Electronic Organs
Upper: Flutes (or Tibias) 16', 4'
Lower: String 8', Reed 8'
Pedal: 16', 8'
Vib./Trem.: On, Fast

Drawbar Organs
Upper: 80 0800 000
Lower: (00) 5303 000
Pedal: 24
Vib./Trem.: On, Fast

Music by Andrew Lloyd Webber
Lyrics by Charles Hart
Additional Lyrics by Richard Stilgoe

© Copyright 1986 Andrew Lloyd Webber licensed to The Really Useful Group Ltd.
International Copyright Secured   All Rights Reserved

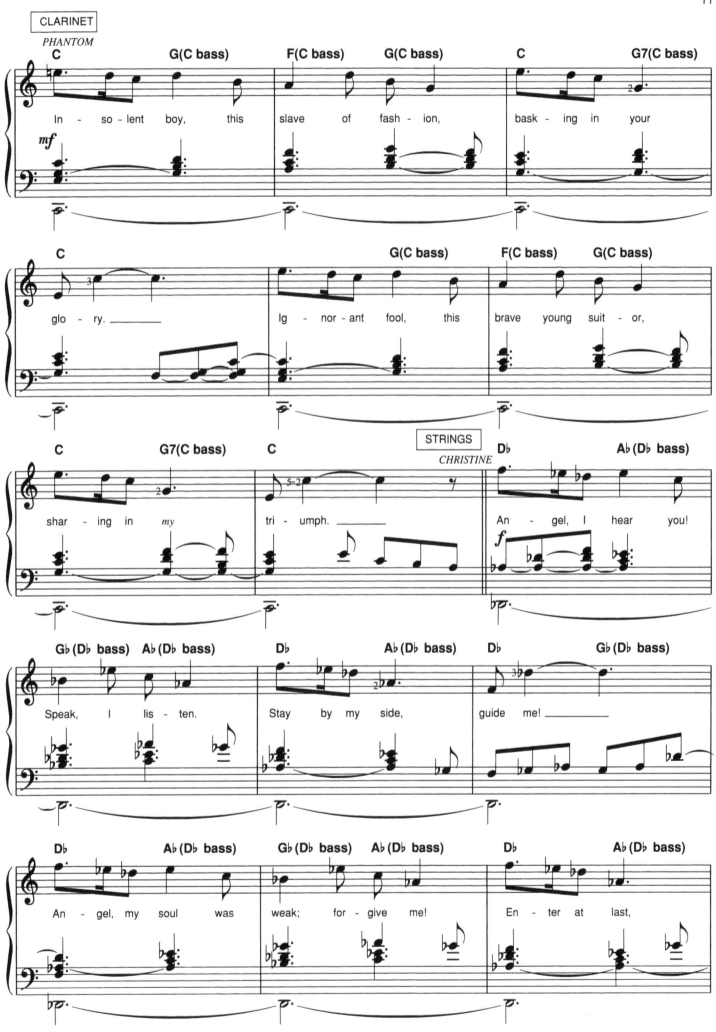

12

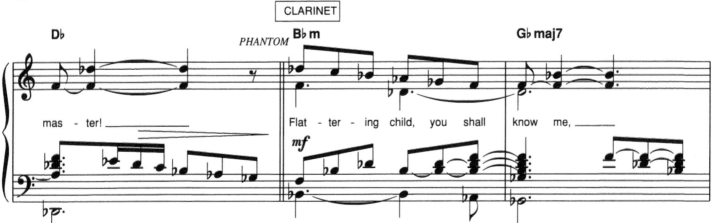

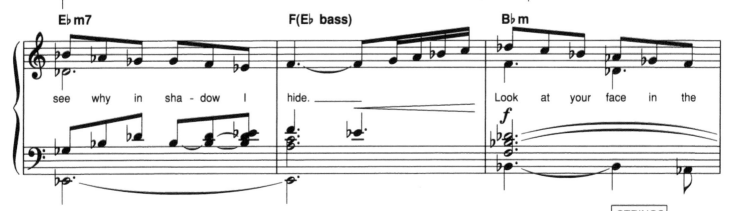

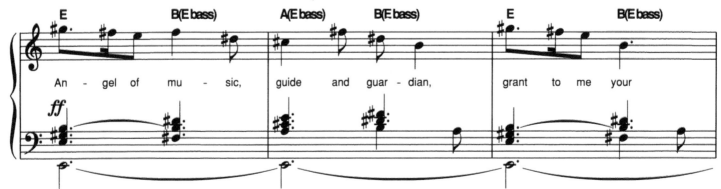

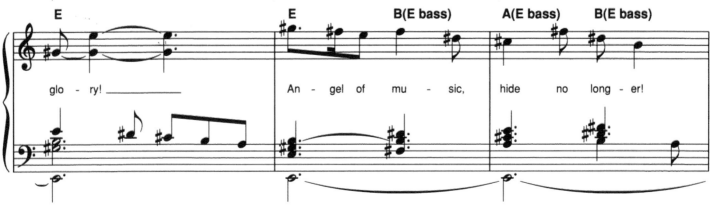

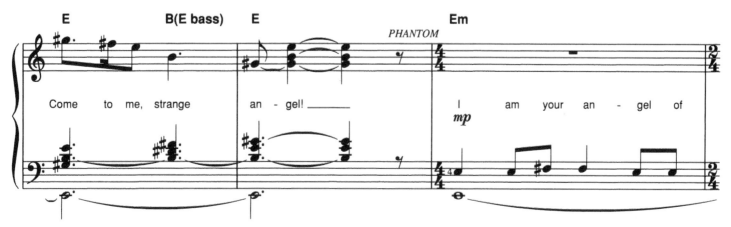

E   **B(E bass)**   **E**   *PHANTOM*   **Em**

Come to me, strange an - gel! _____   I am your an - gel of

mp

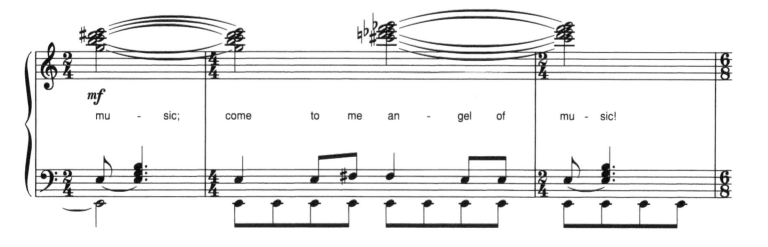

mf

mu - sic; come to me an - gel of mu - sic!

RAOUL   *PHANTOM*
N.C.   **Em**

f

Whose is that voice? Who is that in there?   I am your an - gel of

dim. to end   *ppp*

mu - sic, come to me, an - gel of mu - sic! _____

The Phantom Of The Opera

Electronic Organs
Upper: Flutes (or Tibias) 16', 8', 5-1/3', 4'
Lower: Pipe Organ
Pedal: String Bass
Vib./Trem.: On, Slow

Drawbar Organs
Upper: 42 0026 010
Lower: Pipe Organ
Pedal: String Bass
Vib./Trem.: On, Slow

Music by Andrew Lloyd Webber
Lyrics by Charles Hart
Additional Lyrics by Richard Stilgoe and Mike Batt

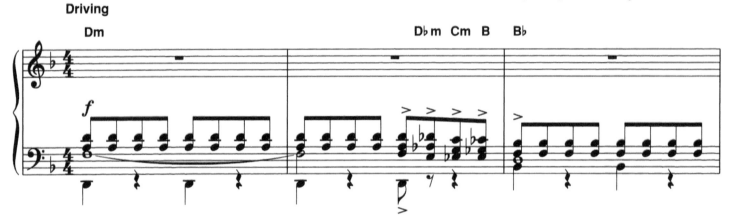

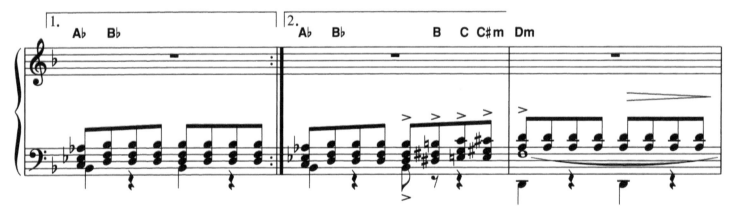

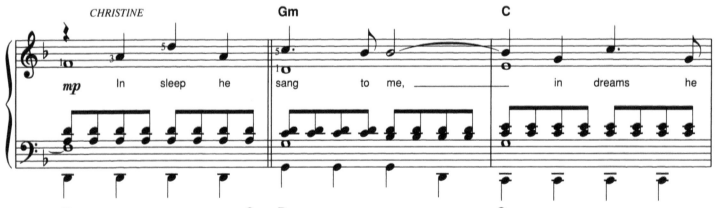

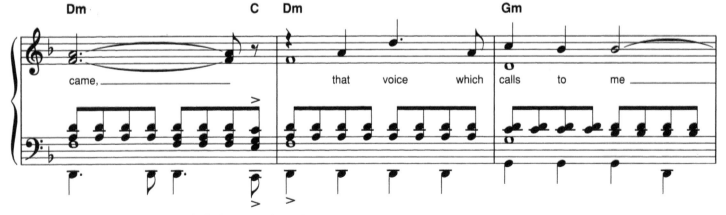

© Copyright 1986 Andrew Lloyd Webber licensed to The Really Useful Group Ltd.
International Copyright Secured All Rights Reserved

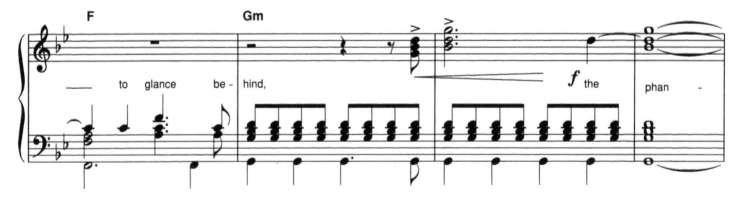

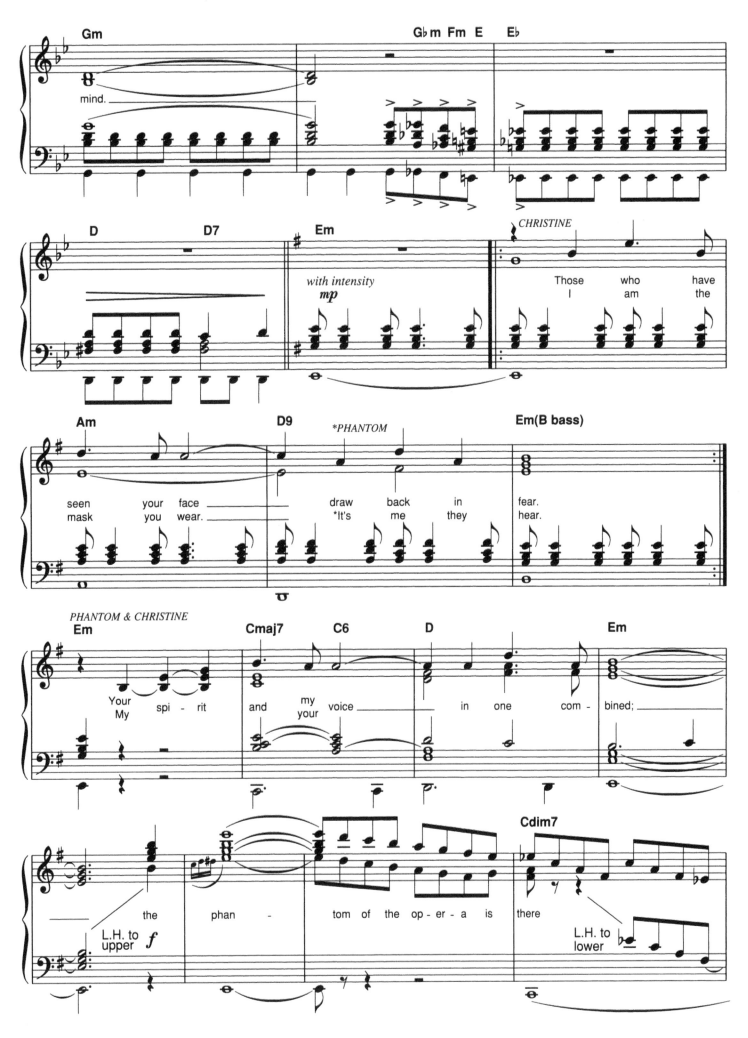

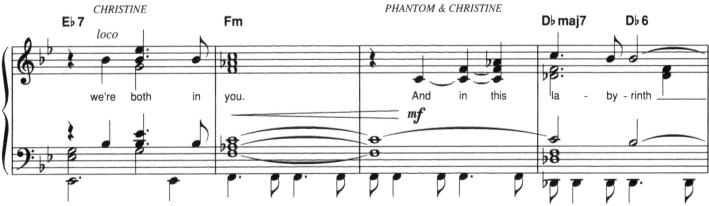

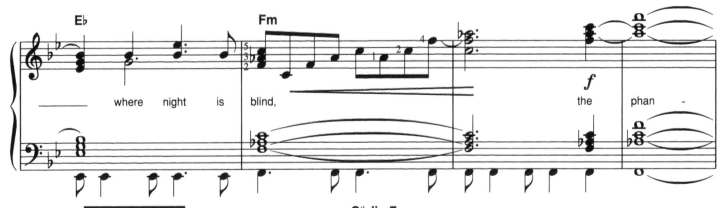

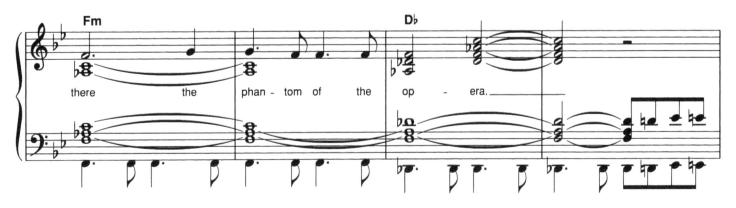

All I Ask Of You

Electronic Organs

Upper: Flutes (or Tibias) 16', 8', 4'
Lower: Melodia 8', Reed 8'
Pedal: 8'
Vib./Trem.: On, Fast

Drawbar Organs

Upper: 80 4800 00
Lower: (00) 7334 011
Pedal: 15
Vib./Trem.: On, Fast

Music by Andrew Lloyd Webber
Lyrics by Charles Hart
Additional Lyrics by Richard Stilgoe

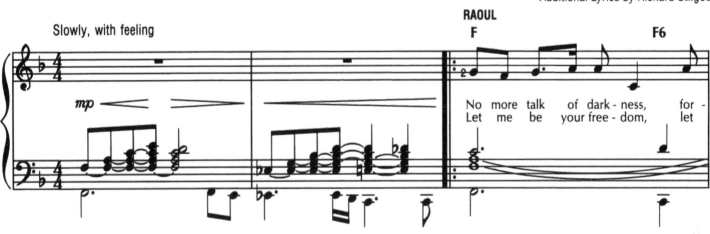

RAOUL

No more talk of dark-ness, for -
Let me be your free-dom, let

get these wide-eyed fears; I'm here, noth-ing can harm you, my
day - light dry your tears; I'm here, with you, be-side you, to

CHRISTINE

words will warm and calm you.
guard you and to guide you.

All I ask is eve-ry wak-ing mo-ment,

© Copyright 1986 Andrew Lloyd Webber licensed to The Really Useful Group Ltd.
International Copyright Secured   All Rights Reserved

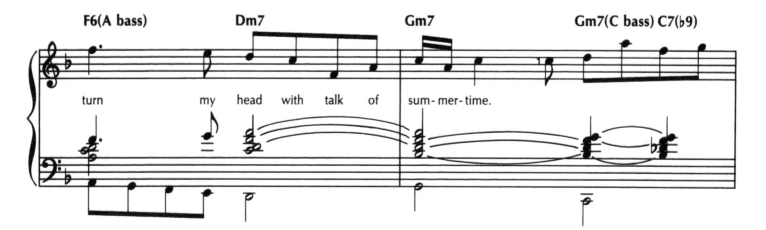

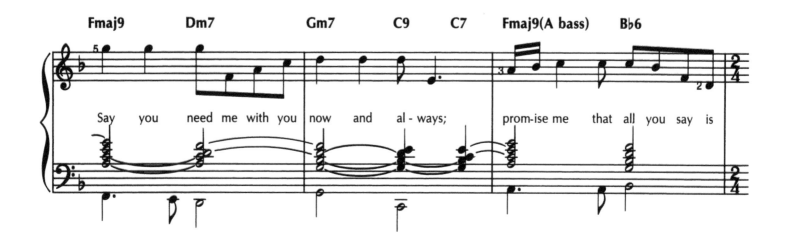

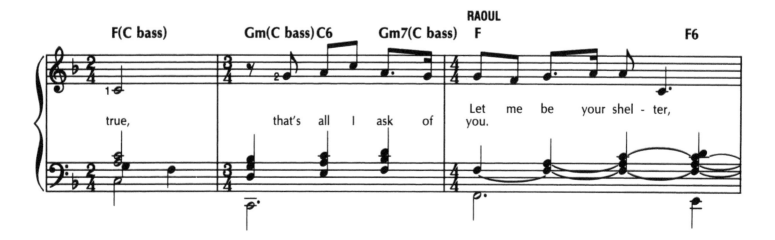

CHRISTINE

Ebmaj7　C9　C7　F6　Fmaj7　F6

fears are far be - hind you. All I want is free - dom, a world with no more night; and

RAOUL

Fmaj7　Bb6　Ebmaj7　C9　C7

you, al - ways be - side me, to hold me and to hide me. Then

Fmaj9　Dm7　Gm7　C9 C7　F(A bass)　Dm7

say you'll share with me one love, one life - time; let me lead you from your

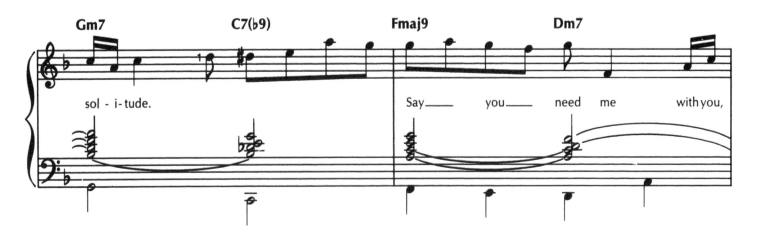

Gm7　C7(b9)　Fmaj9　Dm7

sol - i - tude. Say___ you___ need me with you,

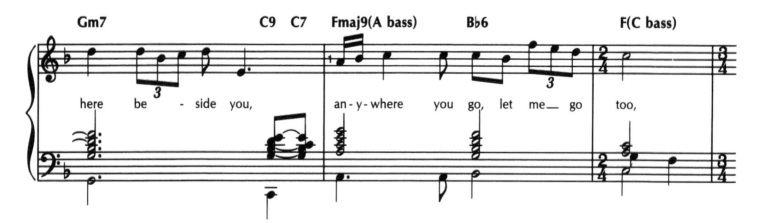

here be - side you, an - y - where you go, let me__ go too,

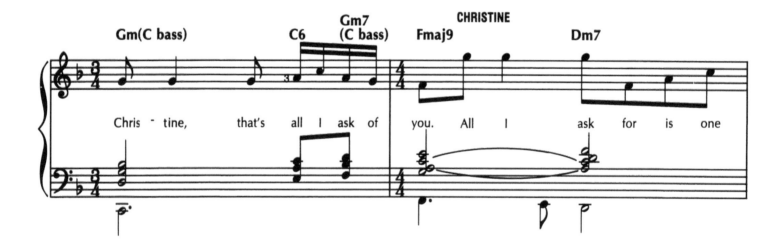

Chris - tine, that's all I ask of you. All I ask for is one

CHRISTINE

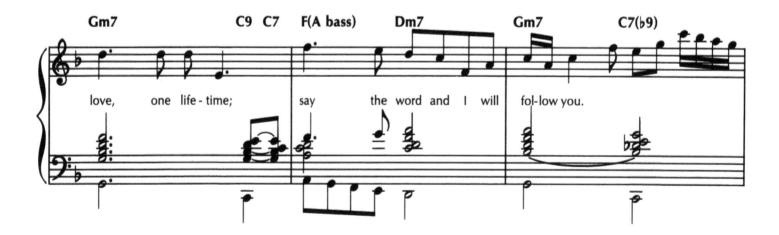

love, one life - time; say the word and I will fol-low you.

RAOUL & CHRISTINE

CHRISTINE   RAOUL

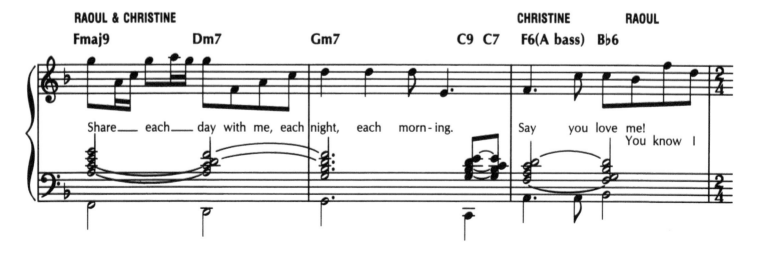

Share__ each__ day with me, each night, each morn - ing. Say you love me!
You know I

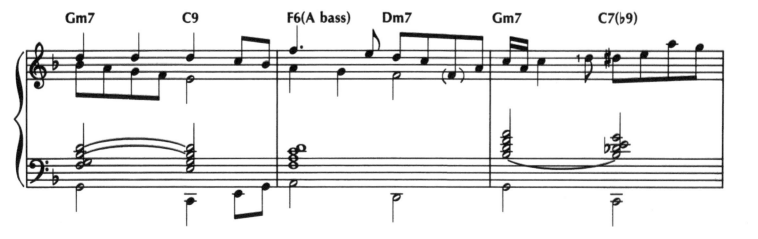

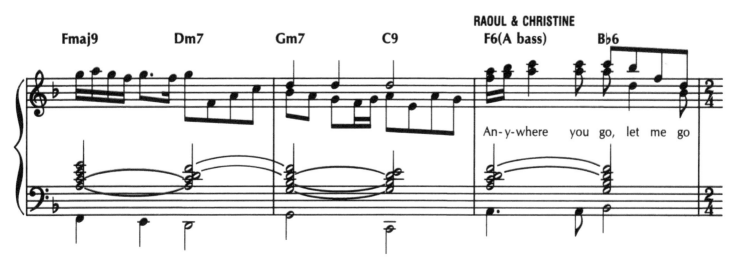

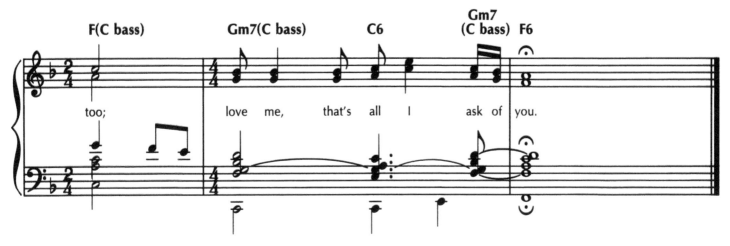

The Music Of The Night

Electronic Organs
Upper: Strings 8', 4'
Lower: Melodia 8', String 4'
Pedal: 16', 8'
Vib./Trem.: On, Fast

Drawbar Organs
Upper: 00 5855 555
Lower: (00) 6500 000
Pedal: 34
Vib./Trem.: On, Fast

Music by Andrew Lloyd Webber
Lyrics by Charles Hart
Additional Lyrics by Richard Stilgoe

Slowly, with intensity

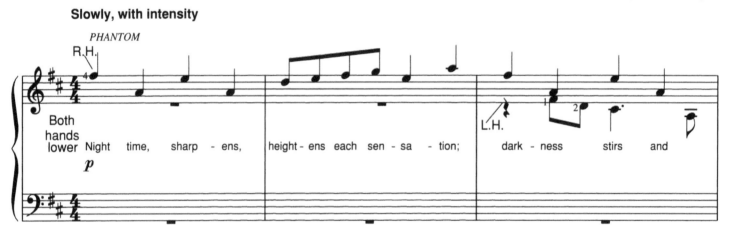

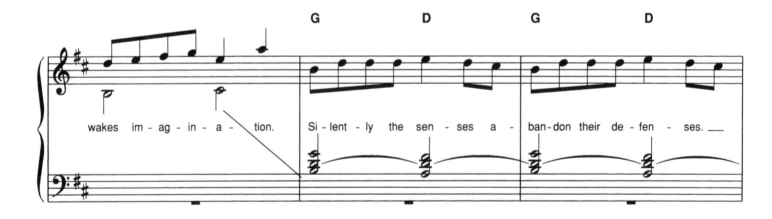

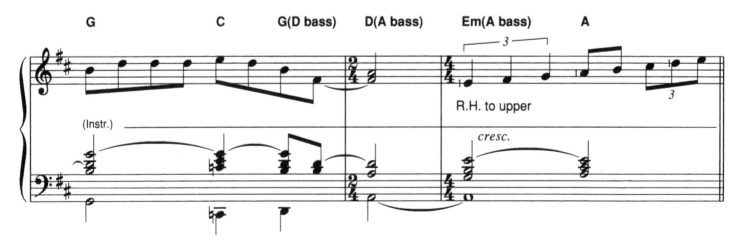

© Copyright 1986 Andrew Lloyd Webber licensed to The Really Useful Group Ltd.
International Copyright Secured All Rights Reserved

D.S. al Coda ⊕

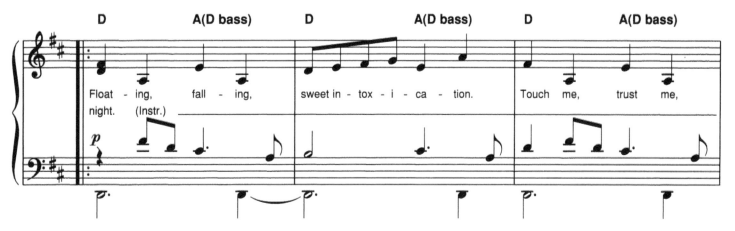

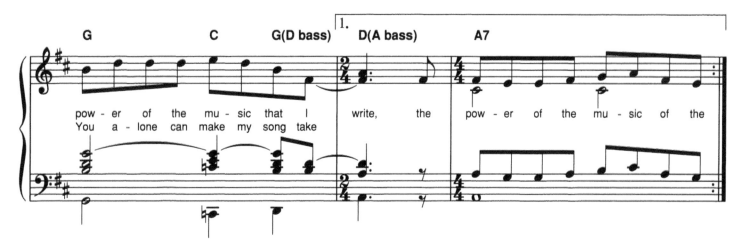

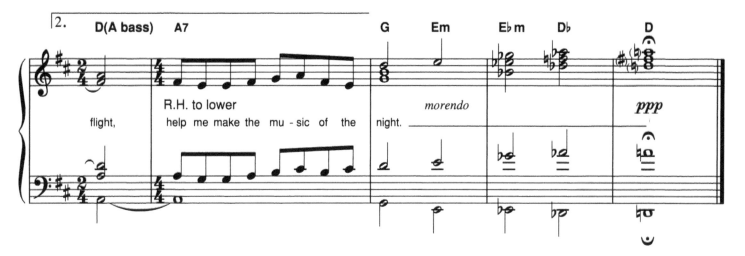

Prima Donna

Electronic Organs
Upper: Strings 8', 4'
Lower: Melodia 8'
Pedal: String Bass
Vib./Trem.: On, Fast

Drawbar Organs
Upper: 80 0801 010
Lower: (00) 5303 000
Pedal: String Bass
Vib./Trem.: On, Fast

Music by Andrew Lloyd Webber
Lyrics by Charles Hart
Additional Lyrics by Richard Stilgoe

© Copyright 1986 Andrew Lloyd Webber licensed to The Really Useful Group Ltd.
International Copyright Secured   All Rights Reserved

REEDS

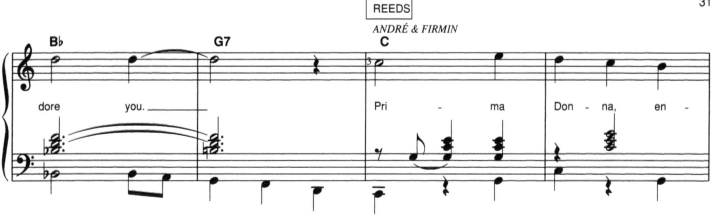

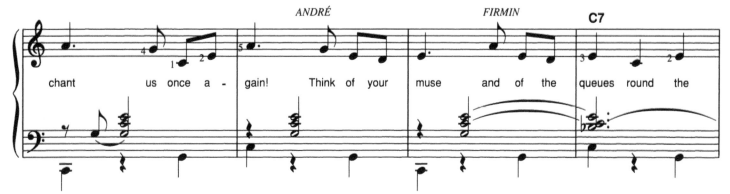

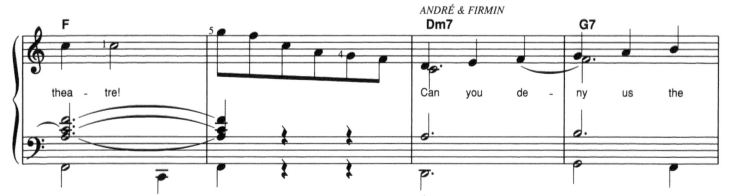

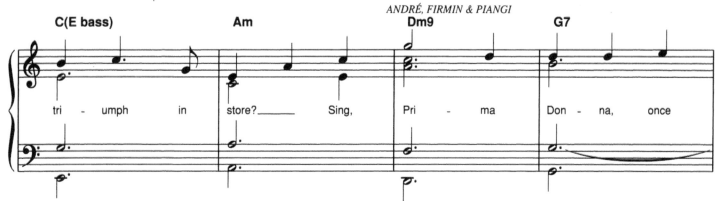

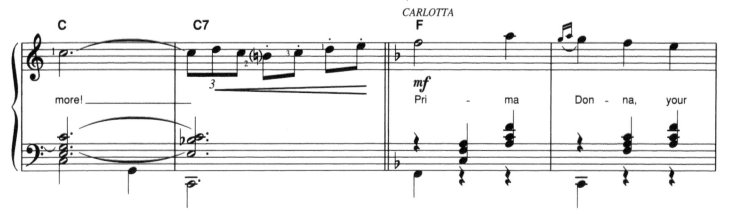

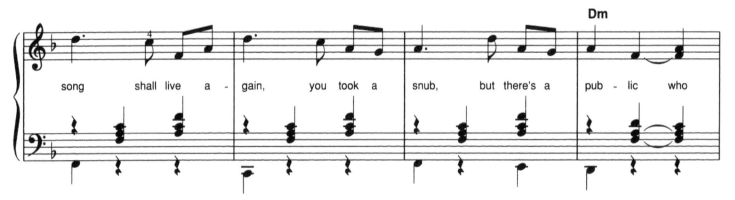

song shall live a - gain, you took a snub, but there's a pub - lic who

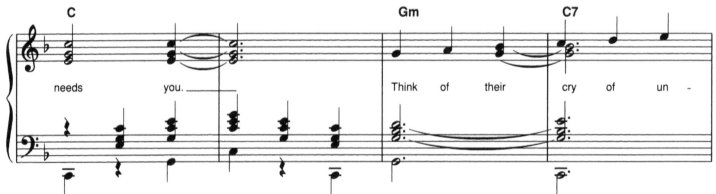

needs you. Think of their cry of un -

dy - ing sup - port, fol - low where the lime - light

FULL ORGAN

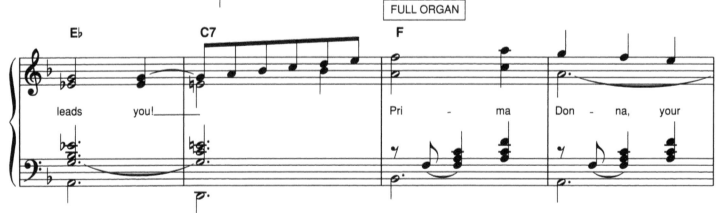

leads you! Pri - ma Don - na, your

song shall nev - er die, you'll sing a - gain and to un - end - ing o -

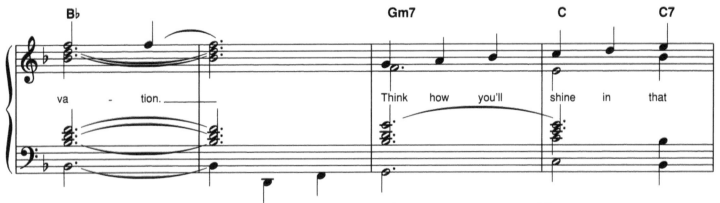

va - tion.____ Think how you'll shine in that

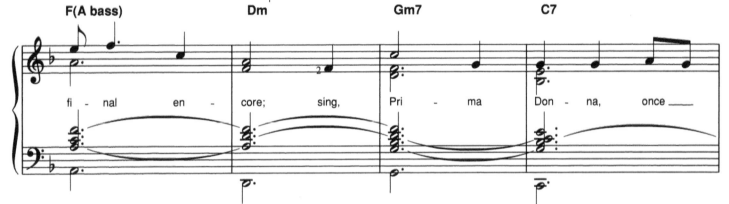

fi - nal en - core; sing, Pri - ma Don - na, once____

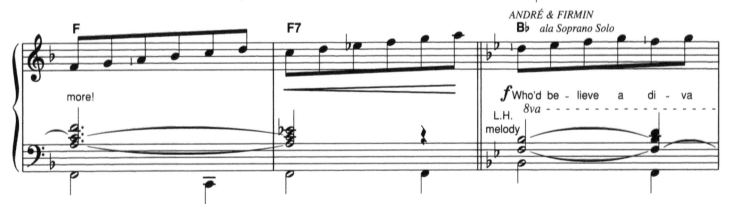

ANDRÉ & FIRMIN

more! Who'd be - lieve a di - va

hap - py to re - lieve a cho - rus girl who's gone and slept with the pa - tron?____

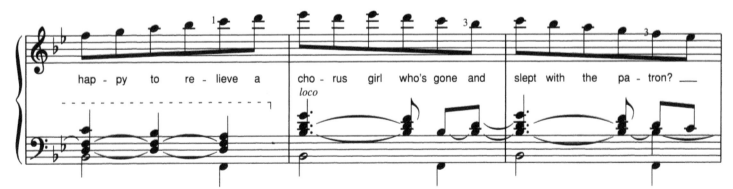

Raoul and the soub - rette en - twined in love's du - et; al - though he may de - mur he

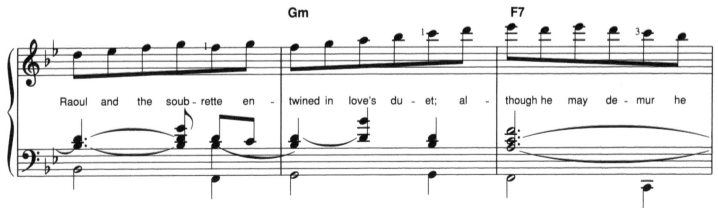

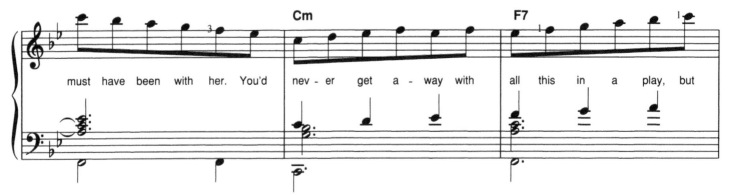

must have been with her. You'd | nev - er get a - way with | all this in a play, but

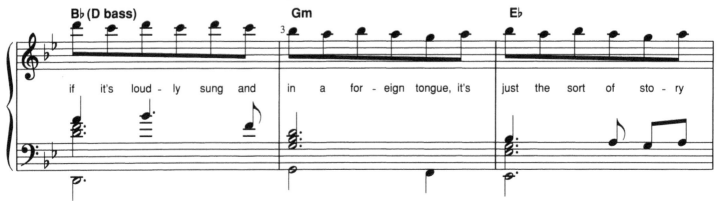

if it's loud - ly sung and | in a for - eign tongue, it's | just the sort of sto - ry

STRINGS

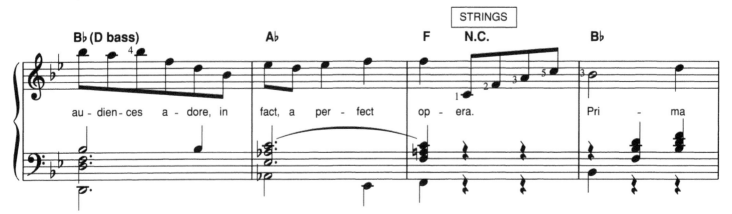

au - dien - ces a - dore, in | fact, a per - fect | op - era. | Pri - ma

Don - na, the | world is at your | feet, a na - tion | waits and how it

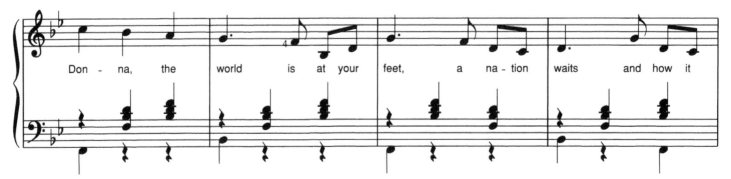

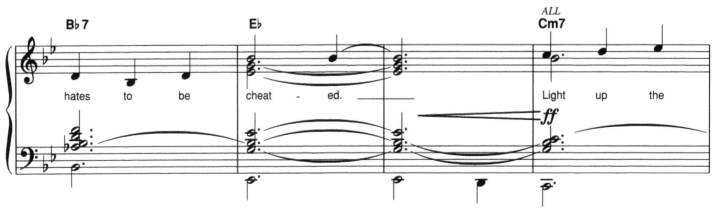

hates to be | cheat - ed. | Light up the

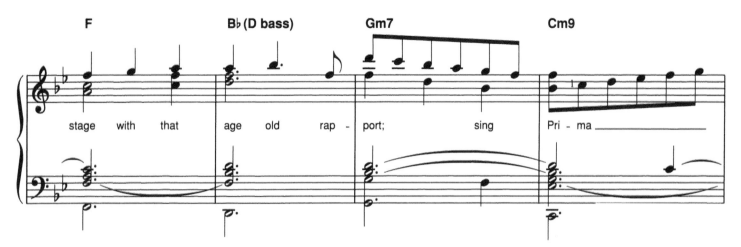

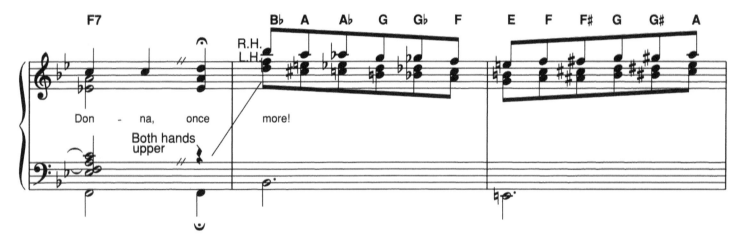

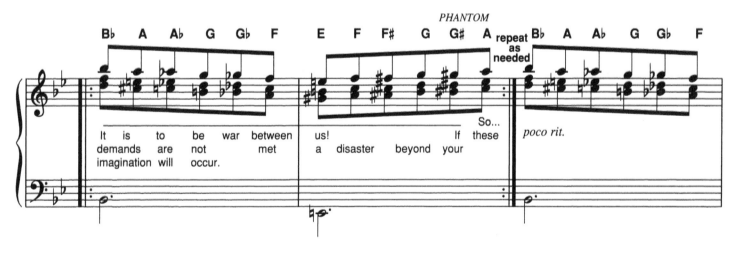

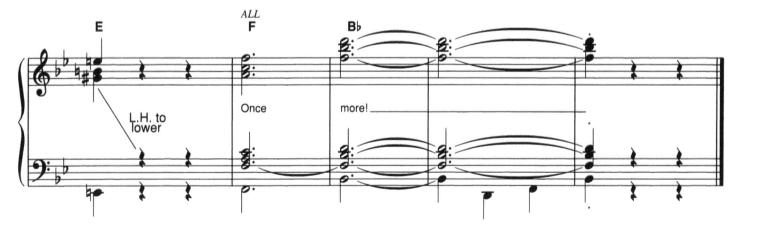

Masquerade

Electronic Organs
Upper: Flutes (or Tibias) 16', 8', 2'
Lower: Melodia 8', String 4'
Pedal: String Bass
Vib./Trem.: On, Fast

Drawbar Organs
Upper: 60 0608 000
Lower: (00) 6500 000
Pedal: String Bass
Vib./Trem.: On, Fast

Music by Andrew Lloyd Webber
Lyrics by Charles Hart
Additional Lyrics by Richard Stilgoe

Quickly, with a "2" feeling

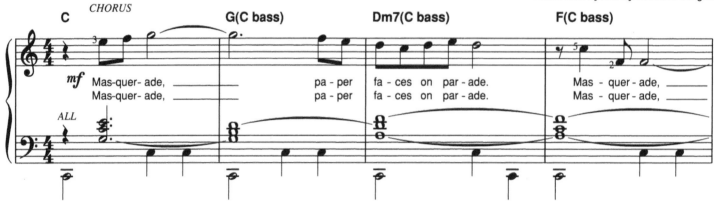

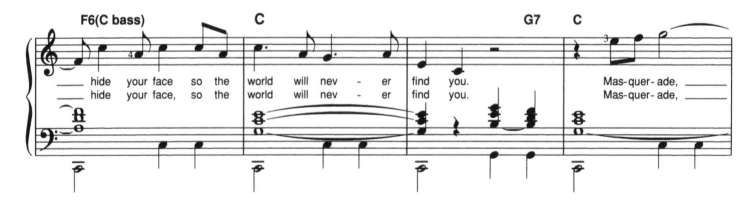

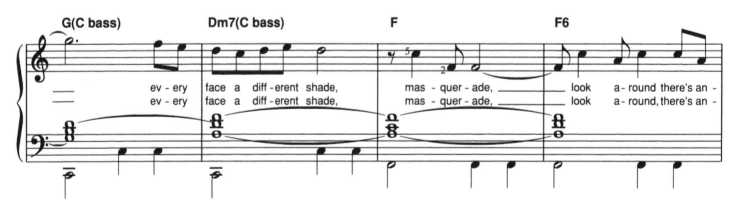

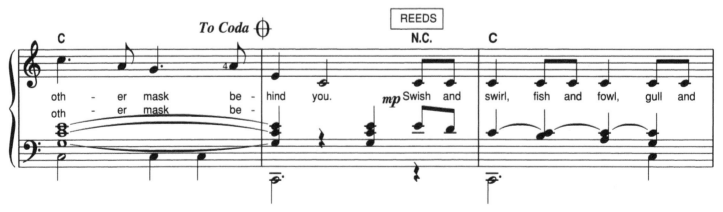

© Copyright 1986 Andrew Lloyd Webber licensed to The Really Useful Group Ltd.
International Copyright Secured   All Rights Reserved

FULL ORGAN

D.C. al Coda

ANDRÉ

bless - ed re - lease and what a mas - quer - ade!

Coda

hind you. Mas - quer - ade, _____ burn - ing glan - ces, turn - ing heads,

Mas - quer - ade, _____ stop and stare at the sea of smiles a - round you.

Mas - quer - ade, _____ grin - ning yel - lows, spin - ning reds, Mas - quer - ade, _____

take your fill, let the spec - ta - cle as - tound you.

Broadly

Wishing You Were Somehow Here Again

Electronic Organs
Upper: Bells
Lower: Strings 8', 4'
Pedal: 16', 8'
Vib./Trem.: On, Fast

Drawbar Organs
Upper: Bells
Lower: (00) 0702 011
Pedal: 24
Vib./Trem.: On, Fast

Music by Andrew Lloyd Webber
Lyrics by Charles Hart
Additional Lyrics by Richard Stilgoe

© Copyright 1986 Andrew Lloyd Webber licensed to The Really Useful Group Ltd.
International Copyright Secured   All Rights Reserved

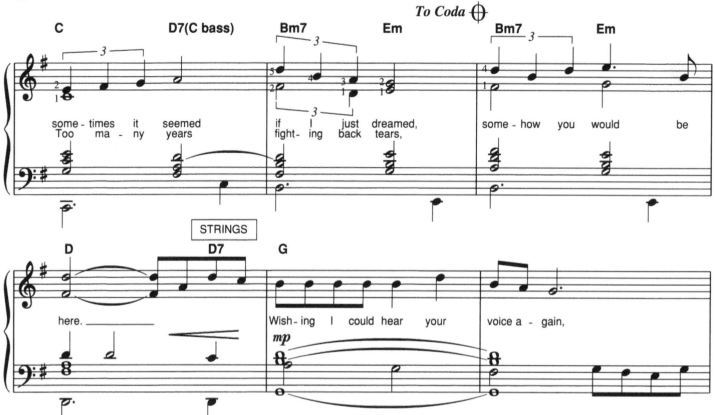

some - times it seemed / if I just dreamed, / some - how you would be
Too ma - ny years / fight - ing back tears,

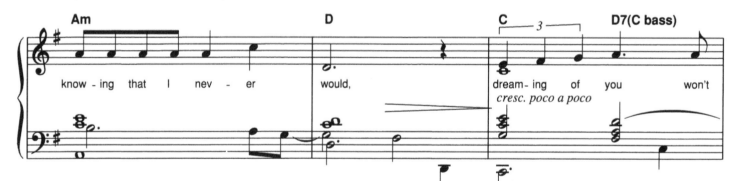

STRINGS

here. _____ / Wish - ing I could hear your / voice a - gain,

knowing that I nev - er / would, / dream - ing of you won't

help me to do / all that you dreamed I could.

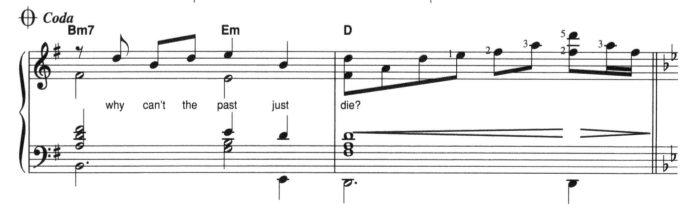

why can't the past just / die?

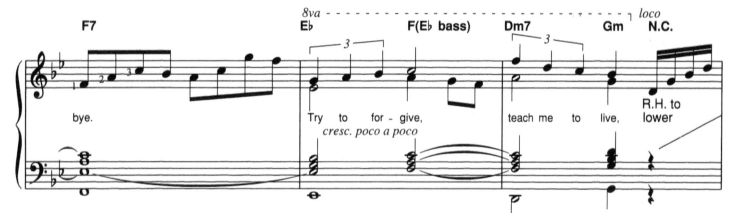

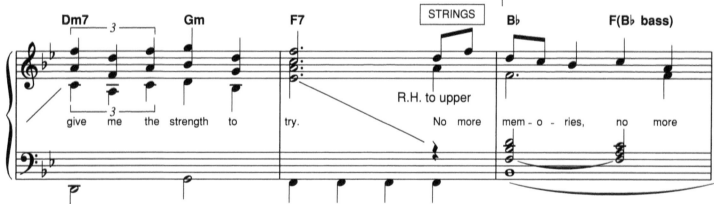

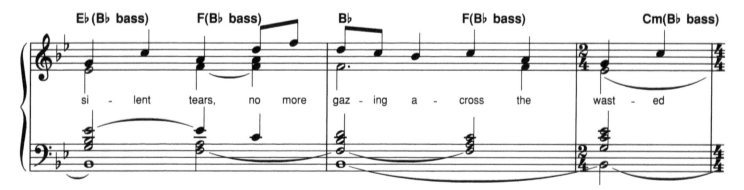

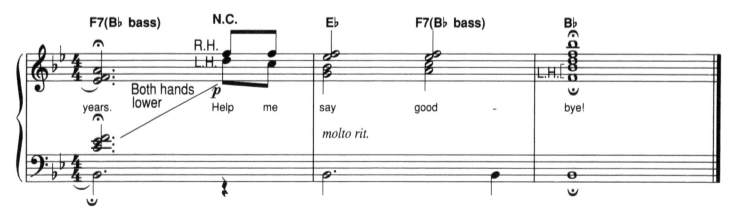

The Point of No Return

Electronic Organs
Upper: Flutes (or Tibias) 16', 8', 4', 2'
     Strings 8', 4'
Lower: Flutes 8', 4', Reeds 8', 4'
Pedal: 16', 8'
Vib./Trem.: On, Fast

Drawbar Organs
Upper: 80 7105 123

Lower: (00) 7314 003
Pedal: 33
Vib./Trem.: On, Fast

Music by Andrew Lloyd Webber
Lyrics by Charles Hart
Additional Lyrics by Richard Stilgoe

© Copyright 1986 Andrew Lloyd Webber licensed to The Really Useful Group Ltd.
International Copyright Secured   All Rights Reserved

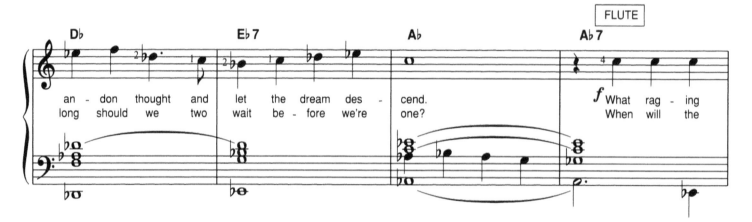

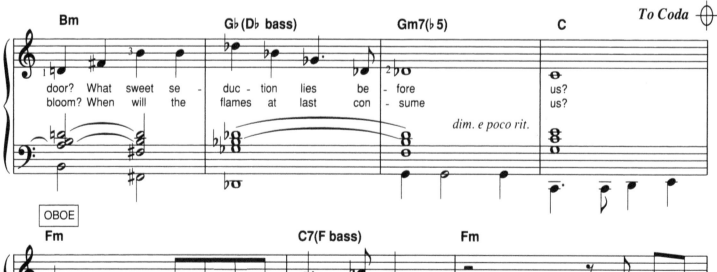

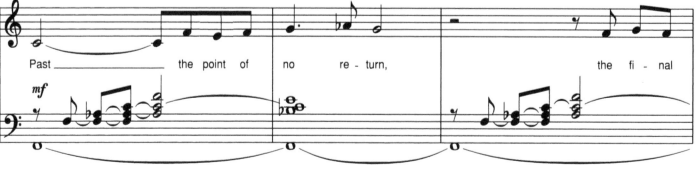

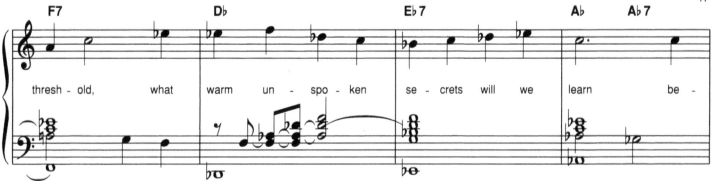

thresh - old, what warm un - spo - ken se - crets will we learn be -

D.C. al Coda

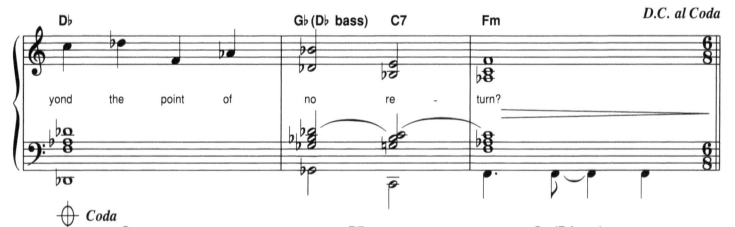

yond the point of no re - turn?

⊕ *Coda*

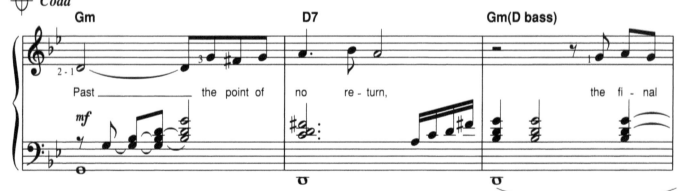

Past _____ the point of no re - turn, the fi - nal

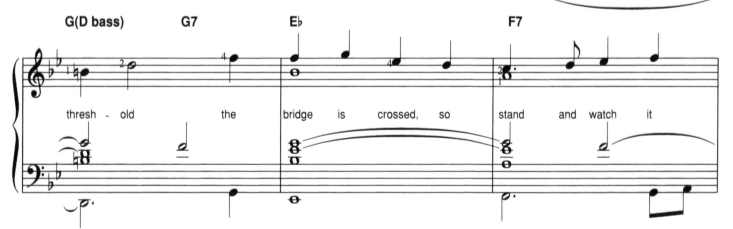

thresh - old the bridge is crossed, so stand and watch it

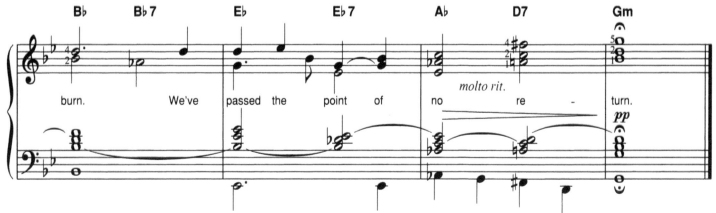

burn. We've passed the point of no re - turn.